CHRISTIAN LEADERSHIP PRINCIPLES FOR YOUNG MEN

Eric W. Barfield

Copyright 2016 Eric W. Barfield

TABLE OF CONTENTS

Introduction: Follow My Example.........................v

Chapter 1: Have Vision Beyond This Friday............1

Chapter 2: Attain and Maintain Perfection..............5

Chapter 3: Avoid Leader Landmines......................9

Chapter 4: Keep Your Oaths...............................15

Chapter 5: Do the Right Thing.............................19

Chapter 6: Be Strong and Courageous.................25

Chapter 7: Dress to Impress...............................29

Chapter 8: Lead by Example..............................33

Chapter 9: Brace Yourself - Setback or Setup?......37

Chapter 10: Loving and Leading a Family............43

Chapter 11: Standing Alone...............................51

Chapter 12: Pursue Continuous Improvement........55

INTRODUCTION

Follow My Example

"Follow my example as I follow the example of Christ."
(1 Corinthians 11:1)

"Don't walk behind me; I may not lead. Don't walk in front of me; I may not follow. Just walk beside me and be my friend."
(Albert Camus)

I spent six years of my life, first through sixth grade, at Banks Elementary School in Kinston, NC where the above quote was hung prominently outside our little school's gymnasium. Yellow letters painted on green plywood that I can still see in my mind all these years later. Not a bad message I suppose for elementary school kids who need to get along but, like the Bible states, "When I became a man, I put the ways of childhood behind me." (1 Corinthians 13:11). So it is with you today.

Christian men have no choice. They must lead. But why Christian leadership for young men? Isn't leadership something for "old" people to worry about? After all, we just really want to play sports (or something) don't we?

Well let me ask you a question. How many of you will be playing at age 20? What about age 30? Age 40? Age 60? Now let me ask you another question. How many of you will be Christian men at age 20? What about age 30? Age 40? Age 60?

The bottom line is that all Christian men are meant to be leaders in some capacity and typically for the rest of their lives. Christian men are to be the leaders of their family. Christian men are to be the leaders in their local church. Christian men are to be leaders in their community. Christian men might also find themselves in many other places of leadership ranging from the president of a small company to the President of the United States.

But why talk about all of this now? Don't we have plenty of time to get to leadership later? Steve Maye is a friend of mine that runs a group called "Lead with Character." When he was a senior at The Citadel, he was tapped to be the Executive Officer, second-in-command of the entire corps of cadets. That in and of itself shows how major leadership opportunities may be thrust upon you in less than five years. But there is another point to make.

Mr. Maye had to report for duty early his senior year and his first order of business was to meet with the Commandant of the Citadel to get his orders for the year. The Commandant told him, "I have one question to ask: Who is your replacement?" Mr. Maye thought his senior year was going to be all about his leadership skill and ability but it was going to be about his ability to teach leadership to others.

The point is that leadership comes sooner than you will be ready so leadership training must come sooner than you would think.

"Follow my example as I follow the example of Christ."
(1 Corinthians 11:1)

Our key verse for this book is designed to remind us that we have both a responsibility to follow Christ and an obligation as Christian leaders to set an example for others to follow.

The verse shows confidence – not in ourself but in the powerful example of Christ. The verse shows humility in that, while leaders, we still are followers under the Lordship and leadership of Christ. And it builds in accountability. If you're not following Christ like you should, time to examine yourself, repent then re-center your life around Christ because others will be watching.

Finally, you can find all sorts of information on leadership – even too much information. However, discovering and learning Christian leadership principles, which is frequently different than secular leadership principles, can be much tougher. This book helps connect the dots between good secular leadership guidance and the ultimate leadership guidance found in God's Word.

Several years ago research revealed the difference between young men in college who drifted away from their Christian lifestyle and the young men who did not. The surprising common denominator among those young men who stayed active and engaged in their faith was the presence in their earlier life of Christian men, in addition to their fathers, who made a meaningful contribution to their character development.

Make sure you connect with at least one other responsible, mature Christian man to help guide you on the pathway to Christian leadership.

Are you ready to step up to the challenge of becoming a Christian Leader?

CHAPTER ONE

Have Vision Beyond This Friday

"For when David had served God's purpose in his own generation, he fell asleep;"
(Acts 13:36)

"Where there is no vision, the people perish."
(Proverbs 29:18a)

"If you get confused in terms of what your mission is, you're not going to accomplish the mission."
(Rex Ryan, NFL football coach)

So many men have no vision beyond this Friday. Yet having a strategic vision for life is fundamental to Christian leadership. Without it, men easily succumb to what writer Stephen Covey described as "the thick of thin things." Blowing through their days, even working hard, yet working hard on things that don't (or won't) really matter. Like a compass, a life vision keeps you oriented toward those things that really do matter – eternal things. And Christian men who lead must invest in eternal things, seeking a greater reward than the temporary trappings this world offers.

Do you view Jesus Christ as a leader? If so, do you think He had a vision beyond this Friday, or for that matter, Good Friday? Consider the following verses.

How is it that ye sought me? Wist ye not that I must be about my Father's business?"
(Luke 2:49 KJV)

"My food, said Jesus, is to do the will of Him who sent Me and to finish His work."
(John 4:34)

"My Father is always at His work to this very day, and I, too, am working."
(John 5:17)

"Jesus answered, 'The work of God is this: to believe in the One He has sent.'"
(John 6:29)

"As the time approached for Him to be taken up to heaven, Jesus resolutely set out for Jerusalem."
(Luke 9:51)

Early on, Jesus indeed had a vision for His life and He resolutely followed that vision straight to the cross. As a leader, He also instilled that same sense of strategic vision in His disciples: "Then Jesus said to Simon, 'Don't be afraid; from now on you will catch men.' So they pulled their boats up on shore, left everything and followed Him." (Luke 5:11)

Left everything. Followed Him. I want it written on my tombstone because not only will it be literally true once I die, I want it to be figuratively true of my life this side of eternity as I seek to fulfill my own life vision: "Eric served God in his time, then he went Home."

Young men, we must understand we are not here randomly. "…all the days ordained for me were written in Your book before one of them came to be." (Psalm 139:16b) "From one man He made all the nations, that they should inhabit the whole earth; and He marked out their appointed times in history and the boundaries of their lands." (Acts 17:26) "For we are God's handiwork, created in Christ Jesus to do good works, which God prepared in advance for us to do." (Ephesians 2:10)

As Christians, our days have literally been ordained from on high and God most certainly has a plan for our lives so we better make sure we don't get confused in terms of our life mission.

To help set a strategic vision for your life, ask this key question: "What kind of man do I want to be?" Most men never take the time to ask this important question and risk living in a continual state of boyhood, dominating hobbies but rarely adding value to eternally significant issues.

Think back about what you've already learned about men in the Bible ("These things happened to them as examples and were written down as warnings for us." - 1 Corinthians 10:11) and identify some Biblical core values - nonnegotiable character traits for your life.

Finally ask, "What's it going to take to get me there?" This will help define your pathway (mission) to achieving that vision. Just make sure that pathway aligns with and does not betray your core values.

> "Character produces enduring leadership."
> (Edgar F. Puryear, Jr.)

Whether realizing it or not, everyone lives their life based first upon their core values (whatever they may be) and allocation of resources (time, money and talents) according to those values. Having an eternal vision and perspective gives you a leadership advantage when it comes time to allocate the resources God allows for adding eternal value to those who share the "boundaries of your land" which is your particular sphere of influence in this life.

What legacy will you leave? Who is or will be better off spiritually because they know you? Don't underestimate your potential and the remarkable influence of one Godly man who steadily, consistently and relentlessly moves forward in life under Providential guidance.

Heisman trophy winner Tim Tebow once said, "The legacy God intended each of us to leave has to do with the impact our lives have had on the lives of others whom He calls us to serve. It has to do with the difference our lives make in the world…Our legacy should be about building in the lives of all those others, doing something for others that will not only last in their lives here, but for eternity." Amen!

"Run the race with eternity in view."

CHAPTER TWO

Attain and Maintain Perfection

"Be perfect, therefore, as your heavenly Father is perfect."
(Matthew 5:48)

"Perfection is not attainable. But if we chase perfection, we might catch excellence."
(Vince Lombardi)

In chapter one, we learned the importance of leaders having a strategic, eternal vision for life. That is, to begin with the end in mind by selecting your destination (what kind of man do I want to be?).

In order to properly frame this vision, we learned leaders must establish some timeless, Biblical core values. These core values act like guard rails on the road that is your unique mission in life (pastor, attorney, pro athlete, etc). These guard rails are designed to keep you from running off the road as you arrive at your destination and achieve that vision.

As our key verse from 1 Corinthians 11:1 reveals, Christian leaders are to set an example. Since we are to set examples, there is one particular core value that is universally true for all Christian leaders that needs to be understood and remembered: Attaining and maintaining holiness.

If you've ever stumbled across Matthew 5:48 above, have you ever wondered why Jesus would tell us to do the impossible? Apart from Christ, perfection is impossible for sure but is it impossible with Christ? I think perfection with Christ is possible but let me explain what I mean about perfection.

Is God perfect? Yes! Is His son perfect? Yes! There is a word used over and over in scripture that describes this perfection and that word is HOLY. Holy means to be set apart but "perfection" gives me a better picture of what being set apart implies.

We live in a fallen, imperfect world separated from a perfect God by our own imperfect choices ("sin"). The only way to restore perfection is with perfection – and only a perfect God Himself can restore us to perfection. Everything or everyone else would come up short. That's the sole reason why He wrapped Himself in the perfect flesh of Christ and came to earth 2000 years ago, taking the punishment for the imperfection of those who have been or will be born again.

In his conversation with Nicodemus in John 3, Jesus tells him no one will see the kingdom of God unless he is born again. Hebrews 12:14 tells us, "Make every effort to live in peace with all men and to be holy; without holiness no one will see the Lord. Now let's do some quick algebra:

If, "See God" = "Born Again"

And, "Holiness" = "See God"

Then, "Born Again" = "Holiness"

Once you are born again, you are holy and that's why Peter has no problem telling us, "But just as he who called you is holy, so be holy in all you do; for it is written: 'Be holy, because I am holy'" (1 Peter 1:15).

A complicated thing to understand about the whole born again / holiness / perfect thing is that it is an ongoing process. I was born again as a youth and therefore was made holy in the past (the church word is "salvation"); I am born again and am therefore being made holy in the present (the church word is "sanctification"); and I will be born again and made holy in the future when Christ comes back (the church word is "glorification").

During this process I need to be frequently reminded of my identity in Christ (holiness) and therefore continually readjust my thoughts, words and deeds to align with this identity. And during this process, I get to make a lot of life choices.

Mount Mitchell is the tallest mountain east of the Mississippi River. It stands at 6,684 feet above sea level in the Black Mountain range of Western North Carolina. Not far from the summit is a tiny spring bubbling up to the surface then flowing down the mountain. This spring is the headwaters of Rock Creek, which flows into the South Toe River.

The South Toe River flows into the North Toe River which becomes the Nolichucky River near the NC / TN state line. The Nolichucky flows into the French Broad River near White Pine, TN. The French Broad flows into the Tennessee River near Knoxville, TN. The Tennessee River flows south into Alabama and then northwest into the Ohio River in Paducah, KY. The Ohio River flows into the Mississippi River and the Mississippi into the Gulf of Mexico south of New Orleans, LA.

Crystal clear at the top of Mount Mitchell, you could drink the cold, pure water straight out of the ground. However, something interesting happens to this water as it flows off the mountain. Have you ever seen the muddy, murky water of the Mississippi River? As this crystal clear water follows gravity and the river currents, it becomes very impure. It has no choice.

As Christian young men, however, you have a choice. Are you going to let the easy, natural tugging pull of the world's "gravity and currents" draw you down to impurity as you move through life? Make up your mind today to choose purity and to keep choosing purity and you will be well on your way to chasing perfection through holy living.

"Religion that God our Father accepts as pure and faultless is this: to look after widows and orphans in their distress and to keep oneself from being polluted by the world."
(James 1:27)

"For God did not call us to be impure, but to live a holy life."
(1 Thessalonians 4:7)

It's important to be reminded that attaining and maintaining perfection is impossible without Grace through Jesus Christ (John 1:17). We are saved by grace, according to Ephesians 2:8-9. But grace is much more than a victory we experience once (salvation). Grace is also our life teacher (sanctification) and our ticket to heaven (glorification). How do I know? The Bible tells me so:

"For the grace of God that brings salvation has appeared to all men. It [grace] teaches us to say 'No' to ungodliness and worldly passions, and to live self-controlled, upright and godly lives in this present age, while we wait for the blessed hope – the glorious appearing of our great God and Savior Jesus Christ, who gave Himself for us to redeem us from all wickedness and to purify for Himself a people that are his very own, eager to do what is good."
(Titus 2:11-14)

In summary, perfection (holiness) is only attainable exclusively through Christ. Have you surrendered your life to Him? If not, why not?

If you already belong to Christ, remember that perfection is a process – you are a holy person in the Lord who still may do some very unholy things. Baseball players had to be taught the game of baseball. They didn't put on the uniform and magically know all the things needed to know to be a baseball player. So it is with holy living. Grace is your coach that motivates you to chase perfection and teaches you to make better choices in this life.

CHAPTER THREE

Avoid Leader Landmines

"Do not be misled: Bad company corrupts good character."
(1 Corinthians 15:33)

"As iron sharpens iron, so one man sharpens another."
(Proverbs 27:17)

"By the time a landmine is uncovered, it is usually too late to get out of the way. When we step on one of the enemy's landmines, the explosion that follows usually has an adverse effect on our relationships with God and with others, as well as our personal testimony."
(Pastor Charles Stanley)

As holy Christian leaders chasing perfection, the enemy will obviously have some landmines or improvised explosive devices (IEDs) ready and waiting, hoping to blow up our testimony and the example we are setting for others. Landmines come in various forms but we're going to examine what I consider to be four deadly "I-eds": Idolatry; Isolation; Idle words; and "I deserve better."

Idolatry

"You shall not make for yourself an idol in the form of anything in heaven above or on the earth beneath or in the waters below. You shall not bow down to them or worship them; for I, the Lord your God, am a jealous God, punishing the children for the sin of the fathers to the third and fourth generation of those who hate Me, but showing love to a thousand generations of those who love Me and keep My commandments." (Exodus 20:4-6)

Have you ever read Thomas Paine's Revolutionary War essay Common Sense? In it, he compared the British monarchy and its hereditary succession to the nation of Israel's insistence upon having a king in 1 Samuel. Thomas Paine described it as "the most prosperous invention the devil ever set on foot for the promotion of idolatry." The Lord's reply to Samuel was interesting:

> "Listen to all that the people are saying to you; it is not you they have rejected, but they have rejected Me as their king. As they have done from the day I brought them up out of Egypt until this day, forsaking Me and serving other gods, so they are doing to you."
> (1 Samuel 8:7-8)

The Bible is full of stories about men trying to live their life without God. That's called idolatry and it's wrong. In fact, God equates it with hating Him (see Exodus 20:5 above). Leaders must understand that idolatry can creep into their life from many directions and even spring from authentically good things.

If you work hard and prosper but get greedy along the way, that's idolatry (Colossians 3:5). If you gain success and notoriety as a leader but become arrogant in the process, that's idolatry (1 Samuel 15:23). It often comes by not heeding Jesus' command in Matthew 6:33 to seek His Kingdom and His righteousness first. If anything or anyone other than the Lord is first in your life, you are rejecting the Lord as your king and worshipping an idol.

Avoid idolatry at all costs but if you find yourself about to step on this IED check your worship. I am not necessarily referring to church attendance, but the "spirit and truth" of your personal worship of the Lord. God doesn't need our worship – we need it – and it is a great way to keep idolatry at bay.

Isolation

"Whoever isolates himself seeks his own desire; he breaks out against sound judgment." (Proverbs 18:1 ESV)

Another IED Christian leaders need to avoid is isolation. For men in particular, isolation often comes naturally. It seems women more easily gather together in community to share the victories and defeats in life. For men, we get so busy and value independence so highly that leaning on other men for support feels like weakness. Yet one of the sure traps for impurity is isolation.

When we are on our own, we are not accountable and free to yield to the inevitable temptations that come our way. Surprisingly, one of the most isolating places for men is church.

Yes, I said church. If we're not careful, we can develop superficial acquaintances at the one place God designed for us to connect with other like-minded brothers for moral, spiritual support. Don't make this mistake. Pray that God would lead you to a handful of close, Christian men with whom you can share your victories and defeats.

"We live in a society of social networks, with Twitter pages and Facebook, and that's fine, but we have contact with our work associates, our family, our friends, and it seems like half the time we are more preoccupied with our phone and other things going on instead of actual relationships that we have right in front of us."
(Kansas City Chiefs QB Brady Quinn, upon the suicide of teammate Jovan Belcher)

"A chord of three strands is not quickly broken."
(Ecclesiastes 4:12)

Idle Words

"O generation of vipers, how can ye, being evil, speak good things? for out of the abundance of the heart the mouth speaketh. A good man out of the good treasure of the heart bringeth forth good things; and an evil man out of the evil treasure bringeth forth evil things. But I say unto you, that every idle word that men shall speak, they shall give account thereof in the day of judgment." (Matthew 12:34-36 KJV)

Leaders must be effective communicators. They must be able to cast vision and inspire. They must be careful they don't let their own tongue or pen (these days, texting, Twitter, Facebook) trip them up. And they must not fall into the trap of gossip but instead "honor the absent" at all times. Famous WWII General Douglas MacArthur stressed the importance of effective words for leaders in a letter to an English professor at West Point in 1939.

"No man can hope to rise to distinction who cannot [present his views in an intelligent manner] and no man, however humble his position, should fail to be able to do so…Without it a man may have the finest judgment in the world, he may be even wise as Solomon and yet his influence will be practically negligible."
(General Douglas MacArthur)

All Christians should be careful of what they say but for Christian leaders, choosing words wisely is of critical importance. When you are in a position of leadership, your words – the way you communicate with people at all – will come under a microscope. This isn't to say that you worry about everything you say. Be a man after God's own heart, aligning your heart as closely as possible with His, then you won't have to obsess as much about what flows out of your mouth or from your pen.

> "If anyone is never at fault in what he says, he is a perfect man, able to keep his whole body in check."
> (James 3:2)

I Deserve Better

The last IED to explore is most sneaky. It is an attitude of entitlement, pride, arrogance, rationalization, excessiveness, revenge, jealously, bitterness, and/or selfish ambition. The common denominator is a symptomatic thought running somewhere through the heart that begins something like this: "I deserve better." You can be sure that if you experience this symptom then nine times out of ten, "sin is crouching at your door."

When you are in a place of leadership, you will often feel you are doing the best you can then be shocked to discover you've not pleased everyone or feel the inevitable sting of criticism that comes with being a leader. In frustration and fatigue, the natural man often responds or reacts with unacceptable behavior as "offsetting compensation." Sadly, some Christian men respond this way too.

If you've not stepped on the landmine of isolation, you may have a close Christian friend who can spot the IED of "I deserve better" about to go off in your life because it often begins to show through – you guessed it – your idle words. If however it's too late, then the antidote for "I deserve better" is immediate repentance and surrender.

> "If you have a fall – mental, moral, or physical – pick yourself up and start over again immediately. If you do, in the long run life won't beat you."
> (WW I General "Blackjack" Pershing)

In fact, as a leader you will have to surrender to the Lord's leadership like never before. Better to avoid this one altogether if at all possible and the best advice for doing so comes from Solomon.

"Above all else, guard your heart, for it is the wellspring of life. Put away perversity from your mouth; keep corrupt talk far from your lips. Let your eyes look straight ahead, fix your gaze directly before you. Make level paths for your feet and take only ways that are firm. Do not swerve to the right or the left; keep your foot from evil."
(Proverbs 4:23-27)

CHAPTER FOUR

Keep Your Oaths

"When you make a vow to God, do not delay in fulfilling it. He has no pleasure in fools; fulfill your vow. It is better not to vow than to make a vow and not fulfill it."
(Ecclesiastes 5:4-5)

"The pilot in command of an aircraft is directly responsible for, and is the final authority as to, the operation of that aircraft."
(Federal Aviation Regulation, Part 91.3 (a))

When I was in pilot training as an 18 year-old, I vividly remember my first flight lesson. I assumed it would be a "ride along" where I would observe the flight instructor as he showed me how it was done. Much to my shock, he put me in the pilot's seat on that very first flight. After figuring out how to taxi to the runway (you use your feet, not a steering wheel) and getting takeoff clearance, I asked him, "Do I just push up the throttle?" I'll never forget his reply: "You're the pilot. Make things happen."

    Leaders make things happen every day. Whether it's a business, a church or a family, leaders put ideas, plans, hopes and dreams into action. Christian leaders have to understand, however, they are accountable not just to other people but also to the Almighty for their actions. That's why when it comes to oath keeping, it doesn't matter how big or little the promise made, if you tell someone you will do something, you do it. If you tell someone you won't do something, you don't do it – pure and simple.

Back in Jesus' day, people must have decided it wasn't too big a deal to break a promise, as long as it wasn't a solemn promise (a vow or oath). That's why I think He clarified the importance of simply being a man of your word:

> "All you need to say is simply 'Yes' or 'No'; anything beyond this comes from the evil one."
> (Matthew 5:37)

Breaking promises is a modern-day epidemic. We live in a culture that no longer values absolute truth but affirms relative truth. Something is good and right as long as it is good and right for you. But the minute it becomes not so good (often described as no longer being "fun") or it doesn't feel right anymore then we believe it's time to explore other options. We jettison promises like empty Christmas boxes that were once full of hope and dreams.

Leaders do not have the luxury of being wishy-washy about promises. Christian leaders in particular must be men of their word – trustworthy and full of integrity. But integrity doesn't start with telling the truth; it starts with fearing the Lord.

> "I put in charge of Jerusalem my brother Hanani...because he was a man of integrity and feared God more than most."
> (Nehemiah 7:2)

Fearing The Lord can be a tough concept for many to understand because we get hung up on the word "fear" and the idea of being terrified of someone who loves you doesn't make sense. But the Bible is pretty clear what it really means:

> "The fear of The Lord is the beginning of knowledge...To fear The Lord is to hate evil."
> (Proverbs 1:7 & 8:13)

To hate evil. Around my house, we say to fear The Lord is "to like what He likes and hate what He hates." Therefore, it's a good idea to "find out what pleases the Lord" (Ephesians 5:10). To fear the Lord is to respect Him and be sensitive to Him – all of His attributes.

Have you ever been at the beach when the waves are really kicking up? To me it is on the one hand beautiful to watch and on the other something I don't want to "mess with" because the powerful current could wipe me out. It's sort of like that when it comes to fearing the Lord.

The reason why fearing The Lord is foundational to oath keeping is because now when you break a promise, you first consider what God thinks about the matter. Great men of the Bible were more concerned about what God thought about their actions than what man thought and how they might please God instead of how they might please men, including themselves.

Paul told the early Christians from Galatia that if he were still trying to please men, he would not be a servant of Christ (Galations 1:10). Filtering your actions this way means you are no longer making your decisions all about what's best for you – and leaders definitely do not make it all about themselves.

The other reason why fearing The Lord is foundational to oath keeping is that you consider what God thinks about the matter before you even make the oath.

It's almost ironic that young men have to make more life-setting decisions before they have the luxury of wisdom built from experience. What to do after high school? What job to shoot for? What woman to marry? More heartache could be avoided in this life if young men honestly sought The Lord about key decisions like this before they "bound themselves with an oath."

But what happens when you find yourself on the losing end of an oath? You've made a promise in good faith but later find yourself a "victim" by the actions or inactions of another or circumstances otherwise beyond your control. Now what? You keep your oath.

But what about when it gets hard? You keep your oath. But what if it means you lose money, power or prestige? You keep your oath.

But what if it hurts? You keep your oath.

"Lord, who may dwell in Your sanctuary? Who may live on Your holy hill? He whose walk is blameless and who does what is righteous, who speaks the truth from his heart and has no slander on his tongue, who does his neighbor no wrong and casts no slur on his fellowman, who despises a vile man but honors those who fear The Lord, who keeps his oath even when it hurts."
(Psalm 15:1-4)

CHAPTER FIVE

Do the Right Thing

"Very early in the morning, while it was still dark, Jesus got up, left the house and went to a solitary place, where He prayed."
(Mark 1:35)

"We are sent here not to be something, but to do something - to do the right thing, It's a big job, and it comes with big challenges. Public service was never meant to be an easy living. Extraordinary challenges demand extraordinary leadership. So if you have come here to see your name in lights or to pass off political victory as accomplishment, you have come to the wrong place. The door is behind you."
(John Boehner, Speaker of the US House of Representatives)

"When faced with a difficult decision, I take the easy way out. I do what's right."
(Hugh White)

We all know we should do the right thing. But there can be two dilemmas in life when it comes to doing the right thing. One is you know the right thing to do but it is so hard to do, it doesn't get done. The other is sometimes you just don't know what the right thing is altogether.

Leaders are selected and expected to make good decisions under difficult circumstances. When it comes to decision making as a Christian leader, you will have to both know what's right - especially when it's hard to figure out. And you will have to do what's right - especially when it's hard to actually do.

Perhaps one of the toughest leadership jobs in the world is President of the United States. The President has to make crucial daily decisions that literally affect millions of people in the US and around the globe. In his book *Decision Points*, former President George Bush summarized how he approached making key decisions.

"I would clarify my guiding principles, listen to experts on all sides of the debate, reach a tentative conclusion, and run it past knowledgable people. After finalizing a decision, I would explain it to the American people. Finally, I would set up a process to ensure that my policy was implemented."

As you can see, there was thought and intentionality to the way he approached making decisions. When it comes to decision making that results in doing the right thing, leaders don't just wing it. There is a thoughtful, deliberate process.

So it is with Christian leadership. There are however two fundamental keys to knowing and doing what's right as a Christian leader but you can't "flat-line" when I state them because so many of you are accustomed to hearing this that you shut down whenever you hear it again: Prayer and Bible study.

Prayer

Early on in scripture, we find prayer being used to help people make decisions. In Genesis 24, Abraham charged his right-hand man with going and finding a bride for his son Isaac. No pressure, right? How did this nameless servant of Abraham approach this huge responsibility? Scripture tells us (verse 12), "Then he prayed, 'O Lord, God of my master Abraham, give me success today and show kindness to my master Abraham.'"

Jesus Himself once had a huge decision to make. He wanted to hand pick twelve men to help revolutionize the world with the gospel of the Kingdom. Look at how He approached that decision:

"One of those days Jesus went out to a mountainside to pray, and spent the night praying to God. When morning came, He called His disciples to Him and chose twelve of them, whom He also designated apostles:"
(Luke 6:12-13)

If God's only Son had to bathe His decisions in prayer, how much more should we? Prayer is communicating (and communing) with the Almighty. Prayer is a gift and privilege for every Christian, regardless of talent, physical ability or circumstances. And one of the most practical ways for us to exercise and express our faith is by praying to the unseen Lord.

Prayer is the often overlooked piece of spiritual armor (Ephesians 6:14-18) and must be one "go-to weapon" for every Christian leader – the sooner you learn how to effectively wield it, the better.

Here are some simple, useful tips when it comes to the prayer life of a Christian Leader. First, get your orders in the morning. Dietrich Bonhoeffer is credited with stating:

"The morning prayer determines the day. Squandered time of which we are ashamed, temptations to which we succumb, weaknesses and lack of courage in work, disorganization and lack of discipline in our thoughts and in our conversation with other men, all have their origin most often in the neglect of morning prayer."

Next, use the "ACTS" model of Adoration, Confession, Thanksgiving and Supplication. This helps develop some discipline in talking to God because we all sometimes struggle with figuring out how to pray without it sounding so random.

So begin your prayers with adoration by letting God know you think He is awesome because He is.

Keep a short account of sin in your life and agree with God on a regular basis by specifically confessing your sins. Thank the Lord that He is faithful to forgive; that His mercies are new each morning; that He has a plan for your life. Don't take for granted the obvious - food, shelter, clothing, family, sports! Then tell Him your specific requests and, yes, while this is about your personal requests, don't make it ALL about you. This is also your opportunity to pray (intercede) for others.

Finally, speak His language. When in doubt about how to talk to God or what to specifically say, use the "language" of scripture. Pray God's word back to Him. The book of Psalms is excellent for this purpose.

Bible Study

That brings us to the other fundamental key to knowing and doing what's right which is to become a student of the Bible. God cares more about truth and lies than winning and losing because God is Truth. Christian leaders have to be on the side of Truth in order to do the right thing and the only way to know which side is the right side is to know Truth. How do we do that? Jesus gave us the key:

"Sanctify them by the truth; Your word is truth."
(John 17:17)

Make up your mind right now that, regardless of how busy your schedule gets, you will commit to being a lifelong student of the Bible. The Bible is the greatest book, written by the greatest author (God), about the greatest person (Jesus), taught by the greatest teacher (the Holy Spirit). 66 books by 40 writers over 1500 years with the same remarkable theme.

We have a tremendous opportunity – and a tremendous responsibility – living this side of the Cross with

His complete Word readily available for us without restriction. Hide God's word in your heart and I guarantee when it comes time to do the right thing, the path ahead will be a little more clear, even if it's not exactly easy.

Prayer and Bible study are two hallmarks of my son's baseball team and for good reason. We pray on the mound after every game as a testament to the power of prayer and as a testimony to others that we believe it actually works. We hold weekly devotions because we believe in the power of the word of God to train young men for their future roles as Christian leaders.

If you haven't already, develop and commit to a lifestyle and love for prayer and Bible study. Passion for these two things is the most effective long-term motivator for doing the right thing.

> "The threat of dire consequences is lousy motivation to do things right. Getting better at something we're passionate about is much more compelling."
> (Frank Robinson, *IFR Magazine*)

CHAPTER SIX

Strong and Courageous – Be Tough!

"Judge for yourself whether it is right in God's sight to obey you rather than God. For we cannot help speaking about what we have seen and heard."
(Acts 4:19)

"The only thing needed for the triumph of evil is for good men to do nothing."
(Sir Edmund Burke, 18th Century British Leader)

I think it might be natural as you get older as a Christian to think Jesus' return must be imminent. I remember my Mom talking about it when I was a kid and even the disciples wrote as if His second coming might be any day and that was 2,000 years ago. But I can't help but be concerned about what's ahead as the relentless march to marginalize the Christian faith rolls on, particularly in America.

As the quote from our last chapter stated, "extraordinary challenges demand extraordinary leadership," one of the biggest challenges of my generation is to prepare your generation for Christian leadership like never before.

Your generation must make a stand for Christ and there will be many who won't do that without solid men of faith showing them how it's done. You need to be one of those men who will stand in the gap when others don't (more about this in chapter 11).

There is a principle in scripture that he who is faithful with a little can be trusted with much (Luke 16:10). When Joshua was given assignment as one of the ten spies to scout out the land of Canaan, only he and Caleb didn't cave in to the peer pressure of the other eight spies' woeful report that ultimately led to Israel's forty-year "time out" in the wilderness. So it's not surprising that God tapped Joshua to succeed Moses as the leader of the Jewish nation after Moses passed away. The Lord's famous charge to Joshua:

"Be strong and courageous, because you will lead these people to inherit the land I swore to their forefathers to give them. Be strong and very courageous. Be careful to obey all the law My servant Moses gave you, do not turn from it to the right or to the left, that you may be successful wherever you go."
(Joshua 1:6-7)

Joshua had a tough road ahead of him and God needed him to be just as tough. As a Christian leader you will have to be tough. There will be times when you will be tested and need to be "shrewd as serpents" and there will be times when it is better to be "innocent as doves." You will see, hear about and likely experience some potentially devastating things in life. You need to be ready for it. As Peter told us:

"Dear brothers, do not be surprised at the painful trial you are suffering as though something strange were happening to you. But rejoice that you participate in the sufferings of Christ."
(1 Peter 4:12-13)

Louis Zamperini was a tough man. Louie competed in the 5,000 meter 1936 Berlin Summer Olympics, catching the attention of Adolph Hitler with his strong finishing kick. In September 1941 he joined the Army as a bombardier on the

B-24 Liberator, flying missions in the Pacific. While on a search and rescue mission for some fellow flyers in April 1942, his B-24 crashed killing eight of the eleven crew members.

Louis survived 47 days adrift in a life raft, including numerous shark attacks and being strafed, before coming ashore in the Marshall Islands. Right into the hands of the Japanese. He was unaccounted for so long that he was listed as killed-in-action yet he survived horrendous treatment as a POW until his camp was liberated in August 1945.

Suffering from severe PTSD and addicted to alcohol, Louis Zamperini gave his life to Christ during a Billy Graham crusade not long after the war. He spent most of his post-war life as an inspirational speaker and even returned to Japan to meet with – and forgive – some of his former captors.

Our generation largely does not comprehend the magnitude of suffering by those who've gone before us, whether it is World War II's "Greatest Generation" or the disciples themselves. But I guarantee there will be at least some suffering as a Christian leader.

The things you've learned about God, including this devotional series, will be challenged by the world. Being faithful to the wife of your youth will one day be challenged. How you decide to educate your children may come under fire. We don't get to choose our trials in this life but when the inevitable times of testing come, remember two antidotes to suffering: Resolve & Rejoice.

Resolve
"But even if you should suffer for what is right, you are blessed. Do not fear what they fear; do not be frightened. But in your hearts set apart Christ as Lord."
(1 Peter 3:14-15)

Rejoice
"However, if you suffer as a Christian, do not be ashamed, but praise God that you bear that Name."
(1 Peter 4:16)

Resolve
"We must obey God rather than men."
(Acts 5:29b)

Rejoice
"The apostles left the Sanhedrin, rejoicing because they had been counted worthy of suffering disgrace for the Name."
(Acts 5:41)

    In both sets of the above passages, we see a pattern of resolving in your heart that you will not break faith and then, when the inevitable suffering comes, instead of having a pity party – rejoice! In Luke 6, Jesus told us that His followers can expect to be hated, excluded, insulted and rejected because of Him. Jesus' advice for that reality? "Rejoice in that day and leap for joy, because great is your reward in heaven."
    So when the chips go down for you, keep looking up! Even if nothing else good happens, you can at least look forward to Christ's imminent, if not immediate, return.

"To the family, Louie was among them still, spoken of in the present tense, as if he were just down the street, expected at any moment."
(Laura Hillenbrand's *Unbroken*)

CHAPTER SEVEN

Dress to Impress – Be Tender!

"Therefore, as God's chosen people, holy and dearly loved, clothe yourselves with compassion, kindness, humility, gentleness and patience."
(Colossians 3:12)

"Young men…be submissive to those who are older. All of you, clothe yourselves with humility toward one another, because, 'God opposes the proud but gives grace to the humble.' Humble yourselves, therefore, under God's mighty hand, that He may lift you up in due time."
(1 Peter 5:5-6)

In chapter six, we discussed the importance of being strong and courageous. As Christian leaders, there will indeed be times when you will need to be tough as nails and must "clothe yourself with strength." (Isaiah 52:1a). But there are also plenty of times when we as Christian men will need to be tender. Jesus called it being "harmless as doves." It is impossible to predict or prescribe exactly when and under what circumstances you will need to be tough and when you will have to be tender.

Fortunately, as Christian leaders we carry with us The Key to helping us figure out when to be which: The Holy Spirit. This is what Christ meant when He guaranteed He would not leave us as orphans (John 14:18). It was what God meant when He told Joshua He would never leave him or forsake him. But we are reminded by Paul in Galatians 5 that, since we live by the Spirit, we must keep in step with the Spirit and not become conceited. In Romans 12:3, Paul reminds us "Do not think of yourself more highly than you ought." So we see that one outcome of being led by the Spirit is humility.

> "The fear of the Lord teaches a man wisdom, and humility comes before honor."
> (Proverbs 15:33)

    One trap of being an athlete is that it sometimes becomes all about you. Despite the encouragement and admonition to make it about team, the spotlight often falls on individual performance. Couple this with our modern, consumer culture and you have a better than average chance of thinking this whole deal called life is all about you. It is not – especially when it feels like it is. Recognizing this takes a tremendous amount of humility.

    Once when we began a Thursday morning Men's Bible study at my church, I learned a good lesson in humility. About a dozen mostly strangers are put together in a small group so on the first morning we go around the circle to introduce ourselves.

    One young man spoke of how he was a student at USC who loved to study the Bible and was looking most forward to going on a mission trip to Africa in the coming months. When the introductions were done, an older gentlemen in the group said, "Wait a minute, aren't you the quarterback for the Gamecocks?" Dylan Thompson dropped his head and said, "Yes sir." Do you know how much humility it takes to not do what he didn't do?

    Who do you think is the best example of Christian leadership in the entire Bible? The answer should be easy but some folks start throwing out a lot of names except Jesus. Jesus is in fact our greatest model for leadership and the reason why our key verse for this book is "Follow my example as I follow the example of Christ." (1 Corinthians 11:1) So what main leadership example did Jesus leave for us to emulate? Humility!

"Jesus knew that the Father had put all things under His power, and that He had come from God and was returning to God; so He got up from the meal, took off His outer clothing, and wrapped a towel around His waist. After that, He poured water into a basin and began to wash His disciples' feet, drying them with the towel that was wrapped around Him."
(John 13:3-5)

Imagine the one and only true "Master of the universe" with all authority and power given unto Him. He can do anything He wants, whenever He wants, to whomever He wants. What does He do? He humbles Himself and becomes a servant. The above image from the Last Supper gives a physical description of what humility looks like while Paul gives us a spiritual description of this kind of humility:

"Each of you should look not only to your own interests, but also to the interests of others. Your attitude should be the same as that of Christ Jesus: Who, being in very nature God, did not consider equality with God something to be grasped, but made Himself nothing, taking the very nature of a servant, being made in human likeness. And being found in appearance as a man, He humbled Himself and became obedient to death - even death on a cross!"
(Philippians 2:4-8)

Humility is an enormous theme throughout the entire Bible. Showing humility is rewarded over and over again in Scripture. What are some practical ways you can show humility? There are a ton but I want to share with you one avenue that I think is key: Meaningful Ministry. This is not just humility and it is not just service. Just like Jesus washing the disciples' feet, it is humility through service. That's being tender.

Early in the Bible, we start to see a pattern of looking after others who have a hard time looking after themselves. God commanded the nation of Israel not to reap to the very edges of their field or to gather up the harvesters' leftovers but rather to leave them for the poor and the alien (Leviticus 23:22). Interestingly, it was this command that led the prominent leader of Bethlehem (Boaz) to notice a young servant girl (Ruth). They later became the great grandparents of David!

In the New Testament, this concept is demonstrated by a great summary verse of what it means to be a Christian today:

> "Religion that God our Father accepts as pure and faultless is this: to look after orphans and widows in their distress and to keep oneself from being polluted by the world."
> (James 1:27)

There's nothing that teaches you to die to self more than to live for and serve others. Even at your young age, look around and you'll see people in need. Why not humble yourself and choose that you will take some time to serve them?

Be prepared for this to look nothing like you expect. Be prepared to get your hands dirty. Be prepared for the very people you serve to not appreciate what you're doing. Be prepared to feel some resentment for those who should have known better than to have ended up in need, yet serve them anyway. You will soon discover that "meaningful ministry is messy" but you'll also be discovering the deep benefits of truly dressing to impress.

> "Clothe yourselves with the Lord Jesus Christ."
> (Romans 13:14a)

CHAPTER EIGHT

Lead by Example

"I have set you an example that you should do as I have done for you."
(John 13:15)

"Follow my example, as I follow the example of Christ."
(1 Corinthians 11:1)

"Similarly, encourage the young men to be self-controlled. In everything set them an example by doing what is good."
(Titus 2:6-7)

In the previous chapter, we looked at the example Jesus gave of being a servant-leader. And while we stated that this life is not about you, the fact is there are people watching. What kind of example are you giving them?

As chaplain of my son's baseball team, I would challenge them all the time about the example they were setting: "When the umpire makes a bad call, do you pitch a fit or are you self-controlled? When it's late in the game and everybody starts to get restless in the dugout, are you still focused or are you goofing off? Do you encourage those around you or mostly just ignore them? Are you man enough to confront a teammate privately when they're off base (figuratively)? Do you let people know you're thankful to be healthy enough just to play the great game of baseball? Do you shine the spotlight on you every chance you get or the Lord?"

There are many leadership traits you could demonstrate as an exemplar but as Christian young men in particular, there is one quality that I challenge you to be an example: Hard Work.

> "For you yourselves know how you ought to follow our example. We were not idle when we were with you, nor did we eat anyone's food without paying for it. On the contrary, we worked night and day, laboring and toiling so that we would not be a burden to any of you. We did this, not because we do not have the right to such help, but in order to make ourselves a model for you to follow."
> (2 Thessalonians 3:7-9)

> "Hard work beats talent when talent doesn't work hard."
> (Tim Tebow)

Did you know that man was designed to work before Adam's sin? Look it up! Jesus Himself emphasized His hard work and the very nature of His mission was to "finish His Father's work." The road to leadership is paved with a significant amount of hard work.

You will not find lazy leaders who are true leaders. This is another generational challenge for us to overcome as our present culture places supreme value on comfort, entertainment and leisure. There is nothing wrong with hard work. As the first African-American USAF Thunderbird pilot once told me:

> "Hard work never killed anybody."
> (General Fig Newton, USAF (Ret))

I have a new hero. His name is Eric Strano, former college catcher for the Rider Broncs. A few years ago I had the privilege of sitting right beside the visiting team dugout for a three-game baseball series between the University of South

Carolina and Rider University. I am a hard person to impress but by the end of the third game, I was so thoroughly impressed by the hustle of this young man that I hung around after the game long enough to shake his hand, tell him he played a great series and that, well, he was my new hero.

At the bottom of the first inning, when his foot hit the top step of the dugout, he literally sprinted to home plate. In fact, at the bottom of every inning he would sprint to the plate whether they were ahead by a run, down by a run or down by several runs.

Strano made a spectacular, crashing catch of a foul ball that everyone in the stadium had given up on. On offense, he kept finding a way to get on base but then his team couldn't get him in to score. You could tell he was disappointed when he ran back to the dugout to gear up - but he wasn't throwing gloves and pitching a fit.

While in the dugout, I could look over and see him stay engaged in what was going on out on the field. Eric Strano was all heart – every play. Now this kid may be the worst unrepentant sinner on the planet but the point is the powerful impact an example of being a hard worker can make. So work hard at what? Let's review five areas where Paul told Timothy to set an example:

"Don't let anyone look down on you because you are young, but set an example for the Believers in speech, in life, in love, in faith and in purity."
(1 Timothy 4:12)

We've discussed speech in chapter three (Leader Landmines) when we looked at avoiding the "IED" of idle words. Remember we said work hard at being a man after God's own heart and you won't have to obsess as much about what flows out of your mouth. We'll cover working hard at Love and Faith in the next chapter. In chapter two (Attain & Maintain Perfection) we reviewed what it means to make the pure choice. Work hard at making pure choices.

So that leaves us with Life. How do you work hard at life? It boils down to attitude. Whether you are mowing the lawn, studying math, taking swings in the batting cage, or whatever it might be go at it "all heart – every play!"

"Whatever you do, work at it with all your heart, as working for the Lord, not for men, since you know that you will receive an inheritance from the Lord as a reward. It is the Lord Christ you are serving."
(Colossians 3:23-24)

The Bible has something remarkable to say about hard work. 1 Thessalonians 4 instructs us to work hard not just to take care of ourselves but also to win the respect of those who are not Believers.

As a Christian leader, your work ethic matters because you represent the Kingdom. You need to do all you can to "live up to the Family name" and that takes hard work. What's your work ethic like? When others see you working, are you winning their respect? Are you working hard for the right reasons? Here are some practical, concise tips to remember:

"All Heart – Every Play"

"Work Hard – Win Respect"

"A willingness to work, study and prepare is essential to success."
(Edgar F. Puryear, Jr.)

"Now we ask you, brothers, to respect those who work hard among you, who are over you in the Lord and who admonish you. Hold them in the highest regard in love because of their work."
(1 Thessalonians 5:12-13a)

CHAPTER NINE

Brace Yourself – Setback or Setup?

"...but we had hoped that He was the One who was going to redeem Israel."
(Luke 24:21a)

"What seems like a setback can often be a setup by God for something better."
(Pastor Brad Ball)

In the famous story of the two disciples on the road to Emmaus told in Luke 24, we see a couple of dejected men suddenly energized by the presence of a stranger who was able to give remarkable insight into what for them had been a devastating turn of events. Jesus actually admonished them for being "slow of heart to believe." You see, they couldn't understand that there had to be suffering before there could be glory.

It looked like a war zone. The C-130s, CH-47s and Blackhawks flew low overhead. Pallets of material were stacked row after row alongside the airport fence that was festooned with all types of debris. We waited in a traffic jam of relief supplies flowing into the city of Gulfport one week after the devastating tidal surge, wind and rain that was Hurricane Katrina.

Television never does justice to scenery whether it's the beautiful scenery of snow-capped mountains or the tree-strewn scenery of lives and property lost before me now. A small team of us had come to deliver supplies and encouragement to a community rocked by natural disaster.

One relief trip led to another then another. On that final trip in July 2007, almost two years after Hurricane Katrina had passed through town – and armed now with the wisdom and insight of living through its rebuilding – a local pastor gave a sermon I'll never forget.

Pastor Brad Ball described that when something horrible happens in your life, it is so hard to see how anything good could possibly come from it at the time. But what we often call devastating, God calls development. And his main message was this: "What seems like a setback can often be a setup by God for something better." I can tell you from personal experience this is absolutely true.

"For You, O God, tested us; You refined us like silver. You brought us into prison and laid burdens on our backs. You let men ride over our heads; we went through fire and water, but You brought us to a place of abundance."
(Psalm 66:10-12)

Global evangelist and former University of South Carolina football chaplain Adrian Despres once explained to me how silver is purified. You essentially boil it in a pot – heat it to a very high temperature which forces all the imperfections, called dross, to the surface. The dross is scraped off the top and the material is re-heated. This keeps happening until the material essentially no longer boils. There is no more dross or imperfections to remove. When you look inside the pot now, it's like looking into a mirror.

The Bible tells me this type testing of my faith produces perseverance and that I've got to let that process finish so that I may be mature and complete, not lacking anything (James 1).

If you remember back to chapter six, we discussed the importance of being tough. That is to be strong and courageous because as Christian leaders you will have to face some tough times in your life. Part of normal day in and day out living as a Christian man is knowing when to be tough and when to be tender. But there may be some potentially devastating setbacks that happen and you need to be ready for that possibility.

"You can't wait for the emergency to practice."
(Advice from a very wise flight instructor)

There are things that occasionally come up in this life that "are not in the brochure" and might shake the very foundation of your soul. The truth is there's not much you can do specifically to prepare because you don't get to choose these trials. They typically come out of left field and at a time when you least expect them.

So are we doomed to a pessimistic life outlook, always waiting for the other shoe to drop? No! Generally speaking there are three things you can do to "brace yourself" for a setback: Persevere in Faith; Persevere in Hope; and Persevere in Love.

Persevere in Faith

Faith is being sure of what we hope for and certain of what we do not see (Hebrews 11:1). In fact, without faith it is impossible to please God (Hebrews 11:6). If you again remember chapter six "Strong & Courageous" one of the antidotes to suffering is "resolve." That's what faith is and that's what faith can do. When you resolve in your heart that you will cling to God with the clutching intensity of a drowning man, no matter what might come your way, that's faith!

Charles Spurgeon once wrote, "When you can't see God's hand, you can trust His heart." Faith is what allows you to trust God's heart. Even when you can't see far enough in front of you to take the next step, you can take it in faith knowing the Almighty is ultimately in control. And even if you only have the faith of a mustard seed, you can trust God no matter what.

"Everything is possible for him who believes. Immediately the boy's father exclaimed, 'I do believe; help me overcome my unbelief!'"
(Mark 9:24)

Persevere in Hope

My company's slogan is "The Power of HOPE." Hope is a present desire with the expectation of future fulfillment. And there certainly is power by hoping in the Lord because the Bible tells us that kind of hope does not disappoint (Romans 5:5).

By persevering in faith, we learned we can trust God no matter what may be going on in our life. But trust Him for what? Trust him that, regardless of trials or setbacks, He can either rescue you from your trials and/or (His choice) work all things out for good, even though you may not see how in the present. That's hope!

"...the Lord knows how to rescue Godly men from trials."
(2 Peter 2:9a)

"And we know that in all things God works for the good of those who love Him, who have been called according to His purpose."
(Romans 8:28)

Persevere in Love

True love perseveres, by definition. The endurance of love is pretty much the summary of the greatest love chapter in the Bible (1 Corinthians 13). As Christian young men, you need to understand the significant difference of "eros" love (feelings of love) and "agape" love (self-sacrificial love).

1 Corinthians 13 deals with agape love and this is the true love that counts. What can happen when you suffer a setback however is withdrawal. You put up a wall around your heart in an effort to defend yourself against the possibility of another setback.

Withholding love is like holding your breath. We were created in God's image to love like He does but if we stifle that, we start to die inside which eventually shows on the outside. Christian leaders must love or else their leadership counts for nothing.

Excellent leaders are often forged through adversity. How you persevere under a setback often determines whether that setback becomes a true setback or a setup for something better that's used for His glory.

"I've missed more than nine thousand shots in my career. I've lost almost three hundred games. Twenty-six times, I've been trusted to take the game-winning shot and missed. I've failed over and over again in my life. And that is why I succeed."
(Michael Jordan)

"Pain is temporary. Quitting is forever."

"Moments like this – and our response to them – define who we are."
(Suffolk County DA Dan Corley, one day after the 2013 Boston Marathon bombing)

"And now these three remain: faith, hope and love. But the greatest of these is love."
(1 Corinthians 13:13)

CHAPTER TEN

Loving and Leading a Family

"Be imitators of God, therefore, as dearly loved children and live a life of love, just as Christ loved us and gave Himself up for us as a fragrant offering and sacrifice to God."
(Ephesians 5:1-2)

"It's like a whole other chamber of your heart opened up that you didn't know existed."
(Shannon Hope, on the birth of his son)

None of you want to have this discussion right now. Having your own family might seem like the distant future with lots of other stuff to do and experience before then. Well that all depends on your definition of "distant."

Before you know it, and always before you feel you're ready, nearly every Christian man on the planet finds himself in the position of family leadership. And it is the one place I guarantee you will actually have to lead.

In the previous chapter, I made the bold statement that Christian leaders must love or their leadership counts for nothing. You don't find this idea in mainstream leadership teaching but I can assure you it's true and it is mainly true in the context of leading your family.

"For though we live in the world, we do not wage war as the world does. The weapons we fight with are not the weapons of

the world. On the contrary, they have divine power to demolish strongholds. We demolish arguments and every pretension that sets itself up against the knowledge of God, and we take captive every thought to make it obedient to Christ."
(2 Corinthians 10:3-5)

I had a lot of worldly ideas and beliefs about women, marriage and family before I came to my senses. When my wife told me she was pregnant with our son Daniel, I was scared straight. Although saved much younger, by the age of 29 I had perfected the art of "nominal Christianity" and made life all about me, bless my heart.

Now I was faced with the reality that I might actually be responsible for another human soul. God used that as my wakeup call to get serious about my Faith, stop playing games with Him and actually start truly surrendering my life to the King. I've been learning how to be a Christian leader of my family ever since.

There could be an entire book written on loving and leading a family. All the topics we cover in this book are "walked out" first and foremost in the context of family. In this chapter, however, we're just going to briefly review your two possible roles as a husband and father.

To say that I feel strongly about these roles would be an understatement. Let me put it this way, if I find out that you one day abdicate your responsibility as a Christian leader in the home and mistreat your wife or your kids, I will hunt you down and get in your face. I'm sick of Christian men disgracing the Name by treating their wives and children like trash – or worse.

The Role of Husband

"Husbands, love your wives, just as Christ loved the church and gave Himself up for her."
(Ephesians 5:25)

Before you get married, you need to ask yourself this question: Am I ready to give myself up for this girl? That is the gold standard of "agape" love, according to the Bible. Look here, "eros" love is easy and I think you can have that kind of love for a bunch of people on this planet. But self-sacrificial "agape" love that endures is what counts.

Are you ready, if needed, to set aside your habits, dreams, desires, preconceived notions of marriage or whatever, in order to love this girl the way Christ set Himself aside and loved and served His church? Make sure your answer is "yes" before you move any closer to the altar.

"It is because the Lord is acting as the witness between you and the wife of your youth, because you have broken faith with her, though she is your partner, the wife of your marriage covenant. Has not the Lord made them one? In flesh and spirit they are His. And why one? Because He was seeking godly offspring. So guard yourself in your spirit, and do not break faith with the wife of your youth. 'I hate divorce,' says the Lord God of Israel"
(Malachi 2:14-16)

Will you remain faithful to the wife of your youth? If I had to pick ONE thing where the last couple of generations, including mine, have dropped the ball in setting a good example, it would be remaining faithful to the wife of our youth. And I don't just mean marital fidelity, I mean faithful in spirit, word and deed.

As a society, divorce has become this automatic get-out-of-jail free card we think we can just use when the going gets rough. And we get to dictate the terms and we get to define the meaning of "rough." Like Jesus said in Matthew 19:8, "it was not this way from the beginning." God hates divorce (see above) and we are to find out what pleases the Lord. That is, to like what He likes and hate what He hates.

> "Be kind and compassionate to one another, forgiving each other, just as in Christ God forgave you."
> (Ephesians 4:32)

Will you love your wife no matter what, especially when you don't "feel" like it? Let's face it. We are all human. Even as holy Christians, we slip and do some messed up stuff in this life. And sometimes the people we hurt the most are the people we love the most. In those instances, we have no choice but to seek forgiveness or to forgive, as the case may be. The Lord commands it (Matthew 6:14-15 & 18:21-22). If you'd like to debate that, take it up with Him.

Forgiveness is the only way out. It's true of the afterlife and it's true of the here and now. Sometimes, you have to beg for forgiveness. And sometimes, you have to lavish it on others.

Can you conceive of a "bridge too far" or a line that gets crossed whereby you won't love your wife anymore? To put this in perspective, is there a bridge too far or a line that you might cross whereby the Lord will no longer love you? And, remind me again, how are we supposed to love our wives? Oh, yeah, as Christ loved the church.

If you walk down the aisle with the thought, "I'll love her as long as she..." then you need to turn around and get this straight first.

The Role of Dad

> "Train a child in the way he should go, and when he is old he will not turn from it."
> (Proverbs 22:6)

> "I don't got nobody, man"
> (Line from the movie *Courageous*)

The movie *Courageous* does a great job of highlighting the desperate reality of an America that is increasingly losing its fathers. The above quote is what one young man said when asked why he got caught up doing no good in a gang. Guys if you don't love your kids at home, they will seek – and usually find – love somewhere else. The problem is it often will be the wrong kind of love.

Don't be an absentee father. Love your kids. Spend time with them. Laugh with them. Make mistakes, own up to them, then ask for their forgiveness. Let them see you are human. Let them see Grace and Forgiveness walked out in your life. Let them see you fight for Truth. Let them see you working hard for the Kingdom. Let them see you struggle with hard decisions. Let them see you put the Lord first in your own life and not be just a "Sunday-morning" Christian. Let them see you loving their Mom like crazy.

In the Old Testament story of Samson, there's great insight into what I think is a proper reaction when you find out you're about to be a Dad. I especially relate to it since my response was similar, as I mentioned above.

"Then Menoah prayed to the Lord: 'O Lord, I beg you, let the man of God You sent to us come again to teach us how to bring up the boy who is to be born."
(Judges 13:8)

Now that's a prayer! I'll go ahead and affirm what you will be thinking if and when you find out one day that you'll be a Dad. Yes, you are totally not qualified for the position! But you know your Heavenly Father and He can guide you even when you don't know what you're doing half the time as a father. So what are some things you can do right now to prepare yourself for loving and leading a family? Here are some ideas.

1. Start paying attention to areas in the Bible that deal with husbands and fathers. What does being a Godly husband look like? What does being a Godly father look like?

2. Start praying for your future wife, even though you likely have no clue who she is. And, yes, your wife should be a

Believer too. Don't fall in love then think you can "convert" her.

3. Stay connected to a local church, even after you leave home. In fact, especially after you leave home. Time to start owning your own faith if you haven't already. When looking for a church home, use the "Hebrews" test. To me the overall theme of Hebrews is "Jesus plus zero equals enough." It typically boils down to the deity of Christ and how a person is saved. If a church teaches anything other than Jesus is THE Son of God (Jesus = God) and the ONLY way to be saved is by grace through faith, then don't attend that church. If a church adds to anything written in the inerrant Word of God (the Bible), then don't attend that church. There are plenty of "disputable matters" where church denominations – or even churches of the same denomination – differ and there's room for grace on these disputable matters that are truly disputable. But avoid churches that compromise on the non-disputable matters.

4. Tithe now and don't ever stop. Start learning how to handle money the Bible way. Finances can be a huge area of family contention so learn to be wise with money.

5. Load as many "arrows in your quiver" as you can before you have the responsibility of loving and leading a family (see 1 Corinthians 7:32-33). That is, get as much education, training, credentials, etc. out of the way as possible now. It is much harder, though not impossible, to do this once you have your own family.

In my opinion, one of the most difficult things for modern man to get right when it comes to loving and leading a family is finding balance. The pace and demands of life are huge. Don't make the mistake of "building bigger barns", especially for the sake of your family. Your family is going to want you more than stuff. Which reminds me, I need to wrap this up so I can spend time with my wife and son!

Like I said at the beginning of the chapter, you will likely find yourself in the position of family leader sooner than you think. Don't freak out as you become a "family man." You will sometimes fail miserably as the head of the household. Trust in the Providence of God who is more than capable of taking care of you and your family.

To find out if you're ready to love and lead a family, give yourself the "Sweet 16 Test" of 1 Corinthians 13 to see if you can honestly write your name in the blanks below!

_____is patient.

_____is kind.

_____does not envy.

_____does not boast.

_____is not proud.

_____is not rude.

_____is not self-seeking.

_____is not easily angered.

_____keeps no record of wrongs.

_____does not delight in evil.

_____rejoices with the truth.

_____always protects.

_____always trusts.

_____always hopes.

_____always perseveres.

_____never fails.

CHAPTER ELEVEN

Standing Alone

"What I want for you is that you seek the Lord. That you trust Him, even if it means you're standing alone."
(Alex Kendrick as Sheriff Adam Mitchell, speaking to his son in the movie *Courageous*)

"When the tide [of opinion] is rushing out of the room, he'll be the one man who's not afraid to go against that tide."
(Robert Francis, former NTSB Member describing a colleague)

"Be on your guard; stand firm in the faith; be men of courage; be strong."
(1 Corinthians 16:13)

I love the story of Nicodemus. That is, the complete story of Nicodemus – not just the most famous one by which we get the most famous verse in the Bible (John 3:16). You see, in John 3, the Bible makes a point to tell us that Nicodemus went to Jesus by night. The implication is that he didn't want his Jewish ruling council buddies to know he was "dabbling with Jesus." Jesus tells him how he must be saved (born again) and the curtain quietly closes on the man who didn't want to be seen in broad daylight with the Savior.

But then we see the curtain rise on Nicodemus again in John chapter 7. This time, he and his cronies have gathered to debate whether Jesus was the Christ, their long-awaited Messiah. The prevailing opinion in the room was that you had to be crazy to believe in Jesus. Then one man, Nicodemus, speaks up and says, "Does our law condemn anyone without first hearing him to find out what he is doing?"

Immediate ridicule from all his buddies follows: "Are you from Galilee too?" That's a huge, embarrassing "slam" on our boy Nicodemus from his peers – the people he's probably spent his entire life trying to impress.

Fast forward to the saddest day in human history, as recorded in John 19. Three crosses with three limp bodies are silhouetted against a setting sun. Two Jewish men on a mission approach the center cross and do what good Jewish men don't do. In front of God and everybody they pick up the lifeless body of another human, Jesus, wrap it with spices and strips of linen then place it in a nearby tomb.

One of those men is Nicodemus. It appears that at the end of this most tragic day only he and Joseph of Arimathea have enough courage to stand alone at the cross. Nicodemus – at long last unafraid of what anyone thinks about his feelings for his Master.

As Christian leaders, I can almost guarantee there will be some "moments of truth" in your life when you will have to take a stand for the Lord and His Kingdom.

And you might be the only one standing.

Standing alone is what got Daniel thrown into the lion's den. And standing alone is what got his three friends into trouble for literally taking a stand for the Lord. Everybody ("all the peoples, nations and men of every language") except Shadrach, Meshach and Abednego was bowing to an image of gold. They wouldn't budge or bow and so were thrown into the fiery furnace.

And while the Lord rescued them too, I think the best point to the story is in the way these guys "manned up" in standing for the Lord.

> "If we are thrown into the blazing furnace, the God we serve is able to save us from it, and He will rescue us from your hand, O king. But even if He does not, we want you to know, O king, that we will not serve your gods or worship the image of gold you have set up."
> (Daniel 3:17-18)

Are you kidding me? What a remarkable statement of faith about their belief in the power of God to rescue them! And at the same time, what a remarkable sign of humility wherein they acknowledged God, in His Providence, may not rescue them but they were cool with that too!

Their confidence in the Lord while all the other "peoples, nations and men of every language" cowered in fear left such an impression on the very king who ordered their execution that he proclaims:

> "They trusted in Him and defied the king's command and were willing to give up their lives rather than serve or worship any god except their own God."
> (Daniel 3:28:b)

As Christian young men you may have already felt the tug of unhealthy peer pressure. I wish I could tell you it gets better. It doesn't. In fact, the next five to ten years of your life may bring some of the most intense, unhealthy peer pressure you've ever experienced.

Many teenagers and young adults have two natural, yet diametrically-opposed, desires coexisting within them: Desperately wanting to be different and desperately wanting to fit in. Add some peer pressure to these competing desires and you have a recipe for making some unwise choices you might later regret. It is in these moments that you must stand firm, even if you are standing alone.

I once got some good advice about how to handle peer pressure. Someone told me that whenever he is introduced to new people, he doesn't let the conversation get too far before he lets them know "where he's coming from" in terms of his faith. He found that as soon as people knew he was a Believer, they were less likely to have conversations about things he didn't like or invite him to do things he didn't want to do.

Another friend told me that when you are surrounded by people who keep leading you down the wrong road it is probably time to "change your playground and change your playmates." Yet another friend of mine often proclaims, "Show me your friends and I'll show you your future."

"All men will hate you because of Me, but he who stands firm to the end will be saved…Whoever acknowledges Me before men, I will also acknowledge him before My Father in heaven. But whoever disowns Me before men, I will disown him before My Father in heaven."
(Matthew 10:22; 32-33)

Job had to stand alone. He lost all his children, all his possessions and his health. Even his wife told him, "Are you still holding on to your integrity? Curse God and die!" (Job 2:9) Do you think in that moment, Job felt just a touch lonely?

Being a leader can be lonely and there are occasions when a Christian leader will find himself standing all alone – maybe even within his own family. Often it is in these moments of standing firm that define the leader.

"Therefore, my dear brothers, stand firm. Let nothing move you. Always give yourselves fully to the work of the Lord, because you know that your labor in the Lord is not in vain."
(1 Corinthians 15:58)

CHAPTER TWELVE

Pursue Continuous Improvement

"Flee the evil desires of youth, and pursue righteousness, faith, love and peace, along with those who call on the Lord out of a pure heart."
(2 Timothy 2:22)

"That which you pursue is that which you value...if you want to become a great leader, become a great pursuer."
(Mike Myatt, *Forbes* Contributor)

We began this book by stressing the importance for Christian leaders to have vision beyond this Friday. That is, to begin with the end in mind and establish a strategic direction for your life, running this race with eternity in mind. The key question to ask was, "What kind of man do I want to be?" That becomes your destination.

So we conclude this book by asking the question, "When do you arrive at your destination?" Not until Heaven! Until then and as you gain leadership proficiency, there's something that will shadow you along the way that you'll want to watch out for: Complacency.

A speaker on pilot professionalism stated, "A good paycheck and a good job is where many high achievers go to sleep." Getting complacent, apathetic and in a rut can happen to some of the best leaders if they're not careful. A pastor friend of mine once described a rut as a "grave with both ends kicked out of it." So true! The minute you get in a rut, I think you are no longer leading.

I'm a believer in proper rest and balance but, honestly, I want to cross the finish line in Heaven tired, bloody, exhausted and just flat-out spent. I can overdo it a lot at times but I can't help but keep "pressing the gas" this side of eternity for the cause of Christ, all the while trying to get better for Him. After all, I won't have any teaching left to do once I get There.

We all pursue something in this life. I love the image provided by 2 Timothy 2:22 above. If I pursue the right things, I will be fleeing wrong things. Don't miss the part that reminds us not to pursue solo but to do it "with those who call on the Lord." A Christian leader must be plugged into a community of Believers. Together we all get better. Remember, "As iron sharpens iron, so one man sharpens another." (Proverbs 27:17)

As we discovered in chapter two, sanctification is all about our journey from the time we become Christians until we are called Home to be with Christ in glory forever. A big part of sanctification is a continuous improvement process for each Believer. Christian leaders should never be satisfied with a stagnant, status quo spiritual life. There is always more to learn, more to improve upon, and more to do for the King.

"It will come about at that time that I will search Jerusalem with lamps, and I will punish the men who are stagnant in spirit; Who say in their hearts, 'The Lord will not do good or evil.'"
(Zephaniah 1:12)

"Seek the Lord all you humble of the earth who have carried out His ordinances; Seek righteousness, seek humility, perhaps you will be hidden in the day of the Lord's anger."
(Zephaniah 2:3)

A television show once profiled an amateur athlete who also served as a fulltime firefighter. At 57 years of age, this man was still in incredible shape. When asked how he stayed in such top physical condition, he said he does 400 burpees a day. (In case you're curious, that's a lot of hard exercise.)

But what struck me was his real reasoning behind such a rigorous, consistent workout: "I never know as a fireman when I may be called upon to save a life so I want to be in the best shape possible." Wow! Christian leaders should have a similar view of their leadership responsibility and therefore a similar determination to stay as sharp as they can so they too might be ready when duty calls.

"Smart leaders understand it's not just enough to pursue, but pursuit must be intentional, focused, consistent, aggressive, and unyielding. You must pursue the right things, for the right reasons, and at the right times...Knowing what not to pursue is just as important as knowing what to pursue...the best leaders pursue being better leaders."
(Mike Myatt, "This One Leadership Quality Will Make or Break You" *Forbes* December 19, 2011)

Jesus constantly challenged His disciples to stretch outside their comfort zones. Just when they thought they had things figured out, He would teach them something new or call them to a new level of service. My pastor calls this "lengthening our reach and perfecting our aim." This is exactly the kind of proactive, always-learning lifestyle that should be adopted to guard against the leadership-killer known as complacency.

# # #

Young men, it has been my privilege to share with you some Biblical concepts on Christian leadership. I do not have all the answers. But the Lord has been so kind and merciful to me and laid on my heart a passion for doing what I can to help train up the next generation of men to stand in the gap and lead out for the Cause of Christ. Being in service for the King is the most frustrating, exhausting, trying, hard thing I've ever done. I wouldn't trade it – or Him – for the world!

1 John 2:6

ABOUT ERIC BARFIELD

Eric Barfield is the founder of Anchor 217 Ministries and also works fulltime in the aviation business. A graduate of Embry-Riddle Aeronautical University, he is a Commercial Pilot and Certified Flight Instructor. In 2015, Eric was conferred membership into the Aviation Insurance Association's Eagle Society for his significant contributions to the aviation industry.

Founded on the premise that Jesus told us to go and make disciples, not just converts, Anchor 217 Ministries exists to support the local church through Biblical teaching and discipleship. Through its ministry of teaching, writing and traveling, Anchor 217 picks up where the evangelist leaves off by forming meaningful relationships with people whereby intentional discipleship can take place.

Eric is an active member of Shandon Baptist Church in Columbia, SC where he teaches a peer-group Sunday School class and previously served as Youth Discipleship 101 Leader and Men's Ministry Director. He's been on several stateside mission trips as well as Taiwan and the Dominican Republic.

For five years, Eric was a cross-country coach and baseball chaplain for Providence Athletic Club. He enjoys reading, riding and running, completing one road bike "century" and five marathons. Eric and his wife Kathy celebrated their 25th wedding anniversary in 2015 and have one son, Daniel, who currently attends Charleston Southern University.

ericbarfield.wordpress.com twitter.com/Anchor_217

Made in the USA
Lexington, KY
25 May 2018